JAMES McBEY'S
MOROCCO

—JAMES McBEY'S—
MOROCCO

Jennifer Melville
photographs by Michael Davidson

HarperCollins*Publishers*

HarperCollins Publishers,
PO Box, Glasgow G4 0NB

First published 1991

ISBN 0 00 435630 6

A catalogue record for this book is available from the British Library

Designed by Lynsey Roxburgh

Printed in Hong Kong

Acknowledgements

I am indebted to the following people: in Britain, William Gardner, Andrew McIntosh Patrick, Martin Hopkinson, Ian McKenzie Smith, Francina Irwin, Robin Evans-Jones and Joan Melville; in Morocco, the late Malcolm Forbes, Joe McPhillips, Clemence Bonnet Mathews, the Cherifa of Wazzan, Mercedes Riera, Mohammed Laaboudi. Special thanks are due to Nancy Eastman.

This book is dedicated to Marguerite McBey, whose meticulous record-keeping and vivid reminiscences enabled *James McBey's Morocco* to be written.

Jennifer Melville
Aberdeen, 1991

Foreword

James McBey had no great love for Aberdeen. His memories of the city recalled the bleak and uncompromising place where he worked as a bank clerk, a job he detested. In spite of McBey's sad memories of his home town he visited often and retained friendships with local people. When he died, his American wife, Marguerite, decided that Aberdeen Art Gallery was the most fitting place in which to house her vast collection of her husband's artistic output. Thus in 1961 Aberdeen Art Gallery became the recipient of numerous prints, drawings, sketchbooks and oil paintings by McBey, as well as a large amount of memorabilia, including the artist's photograph albums. This warm association has continued through the years and as recently as 1988 more of McBey's possessions arrived (literally by the trunkload!) to enhance Aberdeen Art Gallery's now unparalleled archive of this artist's work.

In 1989 Jennifer Melville and Mike Davidson visited Mrs McBey in Morocco. The result of the trip was *James McBey's Morocco*, a book which relates the fascinating story of McBey's Moroccan years. Illustrated with the paintings, drawings and prints which resulted from McBey's prolonged stays there and, with the addition of Mike Davidson's contemporary photographs of Morocco, the book reveals how a visit to present day Morocco can at once take one back to what McBey saw and depicted some fifty years ago.

Without the continued help of Mrs McBey the project would not have been possible. At every stage of its production she has been of great assistance and we are most deeply grateful to her. It is to be hoped that *James McBey's Morocco* will encourage a larger audience to take an interest in James McBey's art and to come to love, as he did, the magical qualities of Morocco.

Ian McKenzie Smith
City Arts Officer
Aberdeen, 1991

Tetuan — What a place this is! All between Asia Minor and the Atlantic has been compressed and distilled, and the essence collected and pressed within four ramparts in Jebbel Dersa, and called Tetuan.[1]

So wrote James McBey of his first impressions of Morocco. For this young artist, brought up on the often bleak north-east coastline of Scotland, the colour, noise and pure foreignness of Morocco held a great fascination. Arriving there in 1912 he felt, quite understandably, excited and elated. Like countless artists before and since, McBey found in Morocco an aesthetic allure and picturesque quality undiscovered on previous travels abroad. After this initial visit during the winter of 1912-13, McBey was to return again and again and, except for the duration of the Second World War, was to spend several months of every year in Morocco from 1932 until his death in 1959. Thus in 1912 began an association which was to last for forty-seven years. During that time McBey produced numerous quite remarkable drawings, watercolours, oil paintings and etchings — an opus which stands today as a testament to one man's abiding love of Morocco and also as a record of McBey's outstanding artistic talent.

James McBey was born in the tiny hamlet of Foveran, near Newburgh, some ten miles north of Aberdeen, on 23 December 1883. The illegitimate son of a local girl who could provide him with only the essentials of a basic subsistence, McBey's childhood was harsh and meagre. He showed little promise at school, though he excelled in geography where his artistic skills were put to good use drawing maps. On leaving school at the age of fourteen, the young McBey was taken on as a junior clerk at the North of Scotland Bank in Aberdeen. During his time in Aberdeen McBey spent every spare minute drawing and working on his etchings, a medium inspired by a book on etching which McBey had discovered in the local library.[2] McBey's mother, Annie Gillespie, became blind at this time, and increasingly cold and distant. McBey's home life was kept together by his maternal grandmother, Mary Torn Gillespie, who showed him the love and affection which his mother had always denied him. Annie committed suicide when McBey was only twenty-two and soon after, McBey decided to abandon his unhappy career in banking and turn to art full-time.

Over the next few years, McBey travelled to England, France, the Netherlands and Spain, where he delighted in spending every daylight hour doing what he liked best: sketching and etching. In the Netherlands, McBey had seen artists working in the open, something which was quite new to him: '...in the afternoon we cycled to Volendam. I had never seen an artist at work till now; here were artists working in the open and unashamed'.[3]

From these journeys McBey created a series of etchings which sold extremely well. The Spanish set especially was highly praised and soon McBey was ranked alongside the other two foremost Scottish etchers of the time, Sir D.Y. Cameron and Muirhead Bone.

Now based in London, the young James McBey soon came into contact with other professional artists. One of them, James Kerr Lawson, was to be of great importance to the future development of McBey's career. Lawson was an expatriate Scot, born in Anstruther, Fife in 1862, but brought up in Hamilton, Ontario, Canada, where his family had settled in 1866. Lawson's father had been disabled for many years and the onus of bringing up the large family had fallen on his mother, a woman ambitious both for her family and herself. Lawson's unconventional background may have struck a chord with McBey, who had also had a childhood dominated by strong-willed women. Unlike McBey, however, Lawson had had a conventional artistic training, first at the Ontario School of Art and later with Luigi Galli in Rome and at the Academie Julien in Paris.

Early in his career Lawson had come under the influence of The Glasgow Boys and through them had been introduced to the subdued tonal qualities and compositional devices of Jules Bastien Lepage (1848–84). Also like 'The Boys', in the late 1880s and 1890s, Lawson had been captivated by the work of James McNeill Whistler (1834–1903) and Lawson's later work, especially his portraits, reveals a great debt to this most influential of nineteenth-century artists. Working with Lawson, McBey, twenty one years his junior, was very much the young student, learning his painting techniques and absorbing his artistic influences. Already a well established landscape and portrait painter when McBey first met him, Lawson provided McBey with a secure footing in the established art world.[4]

1912 was a busy year for James McBey. Following his first exhibition of prints, at Gimpel Fils in November 1911, McBey set off in April for Sandwich, Kent where Lawson had a studio. McBey stayed there for nearly a month, lodging at The George & Dragon Hotel and, using a bicycle for transport, he created five etchings and four drypoints of the Kentish countryside. He was delighted with the landscape there, writing on a postcard to Martin Hardie: 'What a stuff is here! Surely centuries of etchers fashioned this land! I cannot make up my mind where to begin'.[5]

The Dutch influence in the etchings produced at this time is extremely strong, and in *The Skylark* and *The Shower* most of the plate is reserved for a vast expanse of sky. McBey's great admiration for the work of Rembrandt van Rijn (whose prints he collected) becomes more

Plate 1 *The Skylark* 1911 etching.

apparent in these etchings and the Dutch artists' atmospheric skies and low horizons, typified by Rembrandt's etchings — such as his *Landscape with Trees* (1643) — were to become recurrent features of McBey's own landscape etchings.

McBey spent the summer of 1912 in Scotland, visiting his grandmother, sketching the countryside of his childhood and completing two more etchings: *The Foveran Burn*, another Dutch-inspired landscape scene, and *1588*, an artistic interpretation of the wrecking of an Armada galleon which had gone aground on the rocks at Collieston, just north of Newburgh.

In November Lawson and McBey set off for Morocco. The decision to go there was almost certainly Lawson's, who had spent nearly every winter in Morocco since his first visit in 1888. Morocco, and more especially the picturesque town of Tangier was then, as it has been ever since, a favourite artistic colony. For many years the town had been a popular painting spot for several of Lawson's contemporaries: Sir John Lavery (1856–1941) owned a house there and visited frequently. William Kennedy (1859–1918) settled there permanently with his family. Both Joseph Crawhall (1861–1913) and Arthur Melville (1855–1904) had visited Tangier and had brought their North African paintings and watercolours back to Britain where it is almost certain that Lawson and McBey would have seen them. For McBey though, still ignorant of the watercolour technique, the trip was intended to be essentially another etching tour. In fact, from the beginning, it proved to be not just that but a real adventure.

The two artists sailed from Southampton on the 26 November on a Dutch steamer, the *Prinses Juliana*. Two days later McBey wrote a letter to his friends the Bryces, describing the journey in his usual, humorous way:

> We should be off Cap Finisterre just now, but Heaven and the skipper alone know where we are. If you cannot make out the writing don't blame me, for we are driving through a frightful blizzard and the ship is sliding down one green mountain to bury half her length in the next. We have had a devil of a time … You let go of your plate for a moment and down it slides to the bottom of the table. The other people let go of their own to seize yours and back come the whole lot. Past you they go like a regiment of cavalry and disappear over the end of the table. The amount of crockery broken on this trip must be colossal. Talk about Florence! [the Bryces' maid] … An English girl got shot out of her chair and landed in a corner amongst a smother of plates, knives, tumblers, soup, potatoes, petticoats and screams....
>
> We are passing steadily the lights on the Spanish coast and a very dramatic moon is showing off theatrical clouds... Have just heard that we have still aboard the Mayor of Southampton who was our pilot down the Solent. He could not get back to his own boat so had to come with us for the whole journey.
>
> Friday 1.20 p.m. Just now was the first meal when there was a decent muster. Some of the lassies are no' bad looking now that the greenish pallor has worn off ...[6]

The swell left by the storm was awesome, even in the relatively sheltered seas east of the Straits of Gibraltar, and reaching shore proved to be just as treacherous as the journey itself:

> Tetuan is a difficult place to get at, and landing from the boat was not pleasant. It is 45 miles from Tangier over the mountains and there are no roads, only bridle paths, then no

big boats reach it by sea. The Dutch steamer on which I was a passenger went along the coast eight miles from Tetuan, and lay a mile from shore. How we were to get off I was unable to conjecture, for the sea was white with mountainous breakers. Soon a small motor launch put out from the tiny pier. It was a miracle how she survived that stretch of broken water, and every moment we expected to see her swamped. She dodged bravely about trying to get near us, but was beaten back time and again. Then the steamer began to pour a tremendous amount of oil on the waves and the launch was able to approach. She did not seem ever to be nearer the bottom of the gangway than about eight feet. More often the gap looked like 20 feet. There was nothing for passengers to do but to jump, and that we all did successfully. Then we got away from the lea of the steamer, and our hearts were in our mouths at every roll. When I got ashore I learned that only a few days before a launch had upset and drowned 14 passengers.[7]

From where they came ashore, the journey back to Tetuan was equally hazardous. Sitting on donkeys, a mode of travel quite unfamiliar to the two men and one which they found excruciatingly uncomfortable, they set off:

> We started to negotiate a wilderness of mud, averaging in depth from two to eighteen inches. This continued for seven long miles, in fact, until we were at the gates of Tetuan. We passed a semi-Spanish semi-Moorish sentry, then underneath a whitewashed Moorish arch, and at once quaint and strange smells fell on us and welcomed us. Higher and higher we mounted on cobbled streets, narrow and tortuous, past little shops, each containing an Arab like an idol in a shrine, through refuse of all terrible kinds, bumping against mules and asses and their owners, to the Soko. Splashed with mud from hats to soles, we sought our hotel, where everything rose and fell for three days till we managed to find our land legs.[8]

Plate 2 'like an idol in a shrine...'

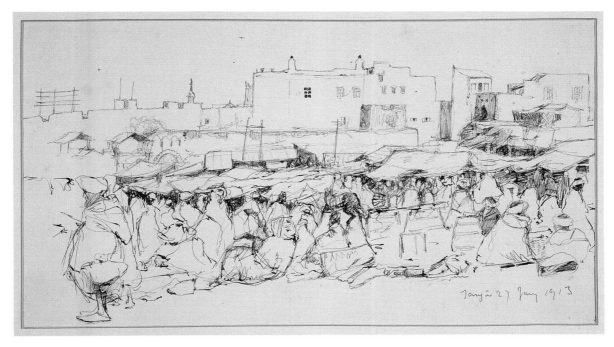

Plate 3 *Moroccan Market, Tangier* 1913 pen & ink.

The two men settled down to their task: Lawson, by now essentially a landscape and topographical artist, to drawing and painting the scenery and buildings in and around Tetuan, and McBey, a lover of action, chatter, gossip and humour, to observing and painting the Moroccan people. He was completely captivated by what he saw:

Since we arrived we have done nothing but stand with mouths agape and codfish eyes, whilst the Arabian Nights have been unrolled before us … It really is a wonderful place. From an artist's point of view the material is unlimited, but I fear it would take years to tap … Today we walked round the outside of the walls. The whole of the Old Testament might have happened here and most of the New also, except, perhaps, Revelation. The voices of Laban and Jacob were raised in dispute; Naaman, the Syrian, was cleansing himself in the river Jordan; Hagar was wending her sorrowful way between the cactus hedges, with the little Ishmael slung on her back… Yonder goes Saul to find his father's asses, and the old fellow who is keenly scanning the distant horizon from the cave behind us is the prophet Elijah.

Returning, we meet one with a tired face, but twinkling eyes, holding a scroll in his hand. Doubtless Solomon thinking out his proverbs. As we near the Soko we hear Tamar on her brother's doorstep, and a lean, brown, wiry unkempt man is vomiting Arabic at his fellows, commenting adversely on the established order of things, John the Baptist!

The lame, the halt, and the withered make up a very considerable percentage of the crowd, and in this land of much prayer and many diverse devils there is no such thing as the unexpected.[9]

13

Plate 4 'no such thing as unexpected...'

It was the lame, halt and withered people whom McBey depicted in a series of etchings. He produced a total of fourteen from the Moroccan trip which divide into two groups. The first group, which comprises *View from the Gate*; *Beggars* (of which there are two versions) and *Gunsmiths*, depict ragged people huddled together in the narrow, covered streets of Tetuan. In the foreground, seated figures wearing *djellabas*, (the distinctive thick wool overcoat of Morocco) crouch, head down, as if sleeping or praying. The murky gloom is pierced by a light in the middle distance which leads the eye through arch after arch to the strong rays of sunlight which stream into otherwise shadowy, sinister streets; a format which at once recalls the etchings of Rembrandt. For James McBey, a man used to the open Scottish countryside, such scenes must have seemed threatening and intimidating. The remainder of the Moroccan etchings depict scenes of open market areas, often with a backdrop of the white city walls and a vast expanse in front, teeming with people, animals and wares for sale. *The Bread Market*; *The Orange Seller*; *The Jewish Quarter, Tetuan*; *A Moroccan Market*; *El Soko* and *The Story Teller* all deploy these devices in slightly different ways.

Of this group of etchings *El Soko* is arguably the finest. In it a busy, bustling crowd is set against a pale, static background of stark, white Islamic buildings, picked out in the winter sunshine. The etching — dated 23 December 1912, McBey's twenty-ninth birthday — heralds his mature etching style. The etched lines are more controlled than in earlier prints and confident strokes capture the scene with great economy of line, achieving a sense of movement and life, sunshine and shadow.

Above: Plate 5 *El Soko* 1912 etching.   Below: Plate 6 *The Story Teller* 1912 etching.

In another Moroccan etching, *The Story Teller*, McBey depicts a subject close to his heart. In those days a professional story-teller was a common sight in Morocco. Standing in the market place, he would attract a crowd by banging an *ag'wal* (drum) or chanting a traditional song to the accompaniment of a *gimbi* (lute). In this largely illiterate society a story-teller was a very important member of the community, not only keeping alive the ancient fables of the society but also relaying more general information and current news. The story-telling tradition was strong in Scotland too, and was familiar to McBey who, with his soft Scottish voice and sense of humour, was himself a fine story-teller. The subject matter might well have reminded McBey of G.P. Chalmers' famous painting *The Legend* (National Gallery of Scotland) which deploys a similar subject, though depicted in the more familiar environment of a Highland cottage.[10] The story-teller as a subject proved irresistible to him. McBey depicted the scene in oil, watercolour, ink and in his superb etching, which stands today as one of the highpoints in McBey's career as a printmaker. In *The Story Teller*, a tall figure wearing a graceful djellaba and pointed hat, is strumming his gimbi and relating his undoubtedly long and complicated tale to the assembled crowd. They sit, huddled against the city walls, watching him and listening to the ancient story. As in all his varied interpretations on the theme, McBey manages to convey a real feeling of suspense. It is as if the climax of the story has been reached and all are waiting expectantly for the denouement to relieve the tension and excitement. Around the story-teller a large space has formed. This open area leads the eye to an Islamic arch, one of the gateways to the city of Tetuan. In the etching (in which, due to the printing technique, the image is reversed) hurried lines scurry across the paper, delineating architectural details and hundreds of figures. The oil painting is simpler, with broad expanses of colour revealing more the contrasts of light and shade than the minute detail of the etching.

A similar confidence is evident in his pen-and-ink sketches dating from this time. A London critic, Malcolm Salaman, had expressed the wish that McBey would further develop this side of his work on the trip: 'a journey which we may hope will result in many characteristic etchings and not a few pictures in oil and water-colours, mediums through which this interesting artist has yet to reveal himself to the art-loving public'.[11] In spite of Salaman's exhortation, McBey had regarded the trip as an etching tour, and it was by chance that he took his watercolour paints too:

As I was leaving the house for Morocco, a bottle of oil, which was insecure in my sketching bag, needed wedging and I seized the first object that came to hand. This happened to be a palette of watercolours; and although I had no intention of working in wash, when in Morocco, I found it very fascinating to put colour over my pen drawing. This is how I came to produce watercolour drawings.[12]

Rather than painting with watercolour, McBey used the colours to wash over his pen-and-ink drawings. This technique of 'colouring-in' with watercolour, instead of painting with it,

Plate 7 *Tetuan* 1913 oil on canvas.
Plate 8 *Study of buildings with Moorish Arch* 1912 pencil & watercolour.

was used by McBey throughout his career. Indeed in later life, when he turned increasingly to the use of oil paints, McBey continued to draw the main shapes in black oil paint, then add colour, in an almost abstract way, with broad expanses of flat colour.

Drawing and painting in Morocco was not easy. The naturally inquisitive people proved to be a problem, solved only with help from a local young man:

Tetuan and the neighbourhood teems with matter for brush and pencil and everyone displayed the curiosity of children. With the utmost sang-froid they would approach and poke their noses — and their fingers if they could — in everything. The Riff youth who carried my materials proved useful for keeping the inquisitive youngsters at a safe distance. His modus operandi was ingenious. The young Riffian had a long stick bound with wire stuck out, and he had no hesitation in throwing this dangerous weapon at children who came too near.[13]

On another occasion McBey was put in a potentially dangerous situation by the Islamic dissaproval of the depiction of the human figure:

I anticipated some difficulty in getting the Arabs to act as models. Their faith prohibits the making of images, and frequently I had to obtain a sketch secretly. The cemetery outside the walls I found a particularly fascinating 'subject', and for days I yearned to sketch it, but could not see how it was to be accomplished without running the risk of getting into trouble. At last I quietly sat down, but had scarcely got the materials out when I was spotted. In a trice there was a crowd of long, lean-jawed, fierce-looking Riffs around me. Each carried an antique flint-lock gun with the charge primed and the hammer at full cock. They were silent at first, and, though I noticed the quick, questioning glances they threw at one another, their undemonstrative attitude made me a little more confident.

At length the awful truth dawned upon them. They became restless, shifting their guns from hand to hand and craning their necks to see what I was doing. Then, with alarming suddenness, they began to talk. Not a sentence was intelligible, but their demeanour spelled trouble. Their voices grew louder and harsher, and their gesticulations more threatening. With one accord the ruffianly crew pressed closer. That decided matters. I had to act, and act quickly. It was the only course. I packed up quickly with as brave and unconcerned a front as it was possible to put on, and with an effort of pretence that they were invisible I walked through the crowd and breathed more freely when the gates were passed. What would actually have happened had they caught me deliberately sketching in this sacred place I do not venture to say; but life is cheap in Morocco.[14]

On 5 January 1913 James Kerr Lawson returned to Britain via Gibraltar, his departure as ungainly as his arrival:

From the Ceuta gate of the town we saw him off in a 'diligence'. This extraordinary contraption is constructed of two packing cases lashed together with string and resting on four supports resembling wheels, three of which are oval and one square. Attached to one end by more string are four skeletons which, owing to their curiously clipped tails, go

Plate 9 *Beggars, Tetuan No.2* 1912 etching.

under the designation of mules. The Spanish driver, having collected into a large box many chunks of rock, mounts the front; Lawson mounts behind, holds on tightly and gives the word to start. The driver then heaves several of the rocks on the skeletons' backs, which causes them to lean forward. The whole thing then begins to move down the hill. It is a queer sensation, when you cannot begin to think of 'safety first'.[15]

McBey spent the next few days sketching in and around the city, and from this time were produced some fine sketches and etchings of distant views of Tetuan.

The following week McBey decided to carry on to Tangier, a perilous journey in what was at that time an extremely dangerous country, where bandits ruled the bridle paths and French gunboats protected the citizens from attack. 'If you do not get a PC from Tangier within the next four days or so, you had better buy up my etchings quickly. This is known on the Stock Exchange as 'inside information', he wrote to his childhood mentor, William Hutcheon [16] concealing his quite natural fear with his usual humour. In the event, his fears proved well-founded:

Plate 10 *Tetuan* 1913 etching.

I had arranged to travel the 45 miles across the mountains by pack mule. The day before I started the British Consul brought me a message to say that the hill tribes had risen, and he pressed me to postpone my journey till the next caravan. However, I decided not to wait and set off next day with a negro muleteer and four laden mules. That night we halted to sleep at a place high on the side of a mountain. Except for losing the bridle paths and making detours to avoid places where the rain had caused landslides, we had nothing exciting to record. Our bedroom was four mud walls, with no roof. When we entered it was already occupied by armed Riffs with their mules and horses. I was the only Christian in the motley crowd. The negro muleteer was the only one to whom I could talk and he was not very communicative. The Arabs appeared to pay us little or no attention, but from time to time I caught them casting glances on the merchandise our mules had carried.

As we spread our rugs on the ground beside our prostrate mules the negro started to talk aloud. I was surprised at his sudden attack of loquacity, but in the light of after events I saw its purpose. 'We start at eight o'clock to-morrow morning' he said to me in a voice that could be heard by everyone. I was satisfied. My muscles were sore with the day's hard

Plate 11 *Approach to Tetuan* 1912 etching.

Plate 12 *Leaf from a Sketchbook — Street scene, Tetuan* 1913 pen, ink & watercolour.

riding, and I wanted a long rest. As soon as my head was down I was unconscious, but I felt I had only been asleep for an hour when a stealthy hand passed over my face. It caught the edge of my rug, turned it down, and shook me by the shoulder. My senses came back with a rush. It was pitch dark. I felt a human breath on my cheek, and then a whisper close to my ear bade me rise. I recognised the voice of the muleteer, but the darkness hid his figure.

'What is the time?' I asked. 'Three hours before sunrise', he said, again in a whisper. 'Well, I shall not get up till eight o'clock', I answered somewhat brusquely, though more cautiously than before, for his anxious tone had impressed me.

'Come', he urged again, 'let us go away,' and I rose as silently as I could and followed him into the night.

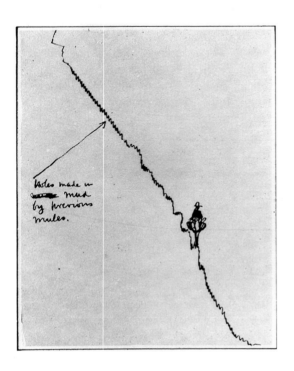

holes made in mud by previous mules.

We roused the mules and packed the merchandise on their backs. It was a weird experience, and my nerves were on edge all the time. The mules kicked the soft earth, the ropes creaked and we tightened the packs, and the sleeping Riffs stirred restlessly. Every sound was exaggerated and seemed to echo and re-echo over the hillside. Cautiously we moved the mules outside, and as cautiously started down the steep path. It was a night like ink for blackness, and as much by good luck as by skilful management we avoided coming to grief. The mules were more mulish than usual, and from down the steep path ahead of me floated the croaking whisper of the muleteer. He condemned, with a wealth and variety of phrases, the ancestors of the stubborn beast he was alternately hauling forward and pulling back.

Plates 13,14 & 15
Journey from Tetuan to Tangier 1912 pen & ink.

The decline was too steep for me to sit as usual on the top of the pack. Sliding and groping with a halter-rope in my hand, I strove to follow the invisible guide ahead… The day dawned and we gained the level. I was caked in mud to the shoulders. My limbs ached with the bruises sustained during the previous day's riding on the morning scramble down the mountainside. I climbed again to the top of the pack and heaved a sigh of relief when safely there. Then I asked the guide what our hurried exit meant. In a word he told me he expected treachery. It may be that his suspicion was accurate. While waiting in Tangier for the boat I heard that the next caravan—the one the Consul wished me to wait for—had been waylaid near the night shelter and two men had been murdered.[17]

In spite of the vicissitudes of the journey, the intrepid McBey continued to sketch, paint and to make preparatory studies for two fine etchings: *The Ford* in which his Berber guide features in the foreground, and *Tangier*. In this etching the two gunboats anchored in the bay are a reminder of how dangerous Morocco was at the time.

McBey found Tangier much more Europeanised than Tetuan, and his lifestyle there was rather more leisured. In Tangier McBey began to sketch fishermen, Riffian women, and the picturesque fortified town, subjects which were to become the basis of his artistic output in later years. The Tangier work has a more sleepy, less frenetic feel than that produced in Tetuan, and this may be a reflection not only of the different nature of the town, but also of McBey's own more relaxed attitude to Morocco as he gradually became accustomed to its foreign ways.

James McBey left Morocco in February 1913. Once back in Britain, he set about the hard

work of printing the etchings from the sketches and notes made in Morocco. He rarely drew directly from nature on to the etching plate, preferring to memorise a scene, and use notes and sketches made quickly on the spot. With the main lines drawn onto the plate, it would be immersed in acid, and, whilst the acid was still biting, McBey would add the finer detail. The etchings are, therefore, not an accurate rendition of what McBey saw in Morocco, but an impression of the sights and sounds that he remembered—a mixture of figure drawings, hurried sketches and his own memory of the atmosphere, action and feel of a certain place and time. McBey did all his own printing: 'When the artist himself prints', he once wrote, 'the printing may be regarded as actually a continuation of his etched work, the combination of both culminating in the finished proof'.[18]

Of the fourteen plates which resulted from his Moroccan adventure, only thirteen were published, perhaps because of his inveterate superstition. As a result, *Road Menders* was left out from the completed Moroccan set, and today exists only as four trial proofs.

Top: Plate 16 *The Ford* 1913 etching.   Bottom: Plate 17 *Tangier* 1913 etching.

The watercolours which had so fortuitously resulted from the trip were spotted lying on McBey's studio floor by a representative of the London gallery, Colnaghi and Obach, and it was there, in February 1914, that the first exhibition of James McBey's watercolours was held. It was a huge success. The London critic, Malcolm Salaman, wrote of the exhibits:

> ... that the manner of these drawings differs materially from the modern accepted idea of water-colour painting, will not be surprising to those who have already recognised the outstanding individuality of this very interesting young artist. McBey never seems to do anything like anybody else; not from any striving after originality, but because he must simply be himself, and a frank expression of his own conception, his own vision, in his own way, is the only thing that would ever occur to him as worthwhile.[19]

Plate 18 *Road Menders, Tetuan* 1913 etching.

In January 1916 McBey was commissioned as a Second Lieutenant and sent to the Army Printing and Stationery Services at Boulogne. Once there, he broke Army rules by continuing to sketch and secretly to record what he saw around him, a habit he found hard to break. The following year Campbell Dodgson, Keeper of Prints and Drawings at the British Museum, recommended him for appointment as an Official War Artist and on 26 May 1917, McBey sailed for Egypt. As in Morocco, he made numerous sketches and watercolour drawings whilst in Egypt, but, once again, the most memorable product of the tour was his etchings, especially those which resulted from a five-day reconnaissance into the Sinai Desert with the Australian Camel Corps. The finest of these is *Dawn — the Camel Patrol Setting Out*, a haunting scene of soldiers on camels riding into a forbidding, yet immensely beautiful, desert landscape.

By the 1920s, McBey was established both in Britain and the United States as one of the foremost painters and etchers of the day. The *Dawn* etching, for which McBey had originally received £3 10s 0d, fetched £445 at auction, the highest price achieved at that time for any print by a living artist.

Plate 19 *Tangier* 1913 pen, ink & watercolour.

Plate 20, 21 & 22 The Marketplace, Tangier 1989.

Plate 23 *Dawn — The Camel Patrol Setting Out* 1919 etching.

Plate 24 Marguerite and James McBey shortly after their wedding in March 1931.

A successful trip to Venice in 1924 resulted in a series of atmospheric etchings of the canals and palaces; Whistlerian in mood, but with the memory of Rembrandt's dramatic lighting still clearly evident. That same year he had an exhibition in New York, where favourable reviews helped to increase his fame. In 1929 McBey visited the United States for the first time. The following year he returned and, based in New York, painted portraits and worked on a series of etchings depicting the city. In November he travelled to Philadelphia, where he had an invitation to paint portraits. On 3 December, he was taken by his friends, the Sesslers, with whom he was staying, to dine with Joseph and Beatrice Winoker. There, he met Marguerite Loeb, a local woman who had been working as a bookbinder in New York. James McBey and Marguerite were immediately attracted to each other. They shared startlingly good looks, a sense of humour and a love of art and, in spite of the large age gap (McBey was forty–eight, Marguerite twenty–five) the relationship flourished. The two were married quietly in New York on Friday, 13 March 1931 and that same day they sailed for Britain.

Marguerite's experience of the British climate had been restricted to two summer visits, in 1922 and 1926. She was quite unprepared for a British winter, and found it deeply depressing:

Every morning as I scanned the sky, looking for a small break in the clouds and beheld only a thick, low, grey blanket I said to whomever was about, 'Do you think it will clear today?' No one had the courage to tell me the truth which I with time found out for myself. When it did clear, it was almost worse, for then I saw that even when the sun does shine, during the winter, it is very weak and has not the strength to stay up long.

Plate 25 *The Artist's Wife Sick* 1932 pen, ink & watercolour.

Plate 26 *Market Scene, Asilah* 1934 pen, ink & watercolour.   Right: Plate 27 Asilah 1989.

James understood my depression and promised to take me to Spain the following winter where he could paint and we could explore the coast to see if we could find a place in the sun—a warm sun. When, after months of adventure, the car finally reached Algeciras on the south coast of Spain, James asked me if I would like to see Morocco. We left the car behind and crossed for a few days.[20]

McBey was deeply disappointed to find the centre of Tetuan quite changed. The old Soko, the Moorish market-place outside the city walls, had been transformed into a Spanish-style town square, complete with palm trees and a bandstand. In order to try to recapture the Morocco which McBey remembered, they decided to travel into the countryside. They took the bus to visit the Sunday market at the remote village of Alcazarquivir, then on to the Portuguese stronghold of Asilah, on the Atlantic coast.

During a two hour wait for a bus Marguerite and James walked around the sleepy fishing village. They were struck by the beauty of this ancient Portuguese fortress, with its eighty-foot terrace and eighteenth century cannons towering above the Atlantic Ocean. The McBeys found a ruined house and spent some time negotiating its purchase. The Spanish Consul was keen for them to have it as it had always been his dream to see an artist installed in this picturesque place. Unfortunately, although it was in Spanish Morocco, the land on which the house stood did not belong to Spain and consequently it was not in the Consul's power to sell it. Today that Consul would no doubt be delighted with Asilah, for it has become a thriving artistic colony, with a cultural festival held every August. The white walls are brightly decorated with modern murals, and, in spite of some unsympathetic modern developments on the periphery of the old fortified town, it remains one of the most picturesque and charming of Moroccan towns.

Plate 28 *Asilah* 1934 pen, ink & watercolour.

McBey Arzila 21 February 1934

The McBeys, unsuccessful in their attempt to buy property in Asilah, returned to the Mediterranean coast at Tangier. The ferry back to Algeciras left at eight the following morning, but McBey woke Marguerite at half-past four, so that they could walk through the peaceful streets and out on to the Marshan, a broad plateau to the west of the town, from which they could see across to the Spanish coastline. As McBey had been on his first visit, Marguerite was struck by the beauty and fascination of Morocco. The couple resolved to return.

The following spring they did return, and immediately set about finding somewhere to live. Remembering the fine views from the hill overlooking Tangier they decided to look there for a house which they could buy. The town had grown enormously since McBey's first visit in 1913 and, as a result of the Convention of Paris in 1923, had become an International Zone, harbouring financiers, smugglers, and criminals. The McBeys found a secluded and overgrown garden on a hillside two miles west of Tangier. In it stood a small dilapidated house, the remains of a summer pavilion which the Cherif of Wazan had built for his famous British-born wife, Emily Keene. Marguerite wrote:

> The day after we had been shown the Cherifa's garden, James said he would like to go to the adjoining hill which looked down onto it for a picnic. In this way we might see it again without giving the impression that we were too keen — a thing to be avoided at all costs. The day was splendid, the view across the water to Spain and then through the Straits of Gibraltar was the most beautiful I had ever seen. There was a serenity and a tranquillity as yet unknown to me ... 'I think I'd like to see what is down there', said James, so we explored the property like a wild park which extended to the sea. We passed into a dark and quiet shade on this day of brilliant sunshine, treading black earth in a world of hushed silence. We traversed groves of giant cedars, large twisted acacias emitting the sweet scent of their yellow blossoms, a stony avenue to the sea lined with old bent eucalyptus trees, a sunny meadow on to the western cliffs where we found a grove of umbrella pines — their trunks like columns — pillars of a mosque against the deep blue of the sea below. Looking west from the cliffside, the whole coast of Northern Africa to its most northwesterly point lay before us. Cistus, broom and great outcrops of the mother rock adorned it ... James loved it immediately and decided to make it his own. So sure was he of his decision that when he came to a glade of mimosas and found an old man and a boy cutting the old twisted trees in full bloom which had fallen, he begged him to delay the work for a few days.[21]

The McBeys managed to purchase both the garden, with its house, and the nearby land, which totalled about thirty acres. They named the house Jalobey, an amalgamation of their two names which sounded vaguely Arabic and, since it was part of the old Cherif's estate, they called the land Cherifian Rocks.

Jalobey was on very fertile land and, nestling on the lea of the Old Mountain, was sheltered from the prevailing east wind. The land around had many deep wells, some of which led into a large goldfish pond which formed the nucleus of Jalobey's garden. It bubbled from a marble fountain into a 35-foot-square tiled pool which was enclosed in the walls of the house. It ran all through the garden in open canals. The garden, about two acres, was a tangle of gnarled fruit trees which, we were to learn, no Mohammedan would prune. Pruning a fruit tree was regarded with the same horror as birth control... an offence against God. There was an astounding variety of vegetation in that garden — a sort of Noah's ark of almond trees, figs, persimmons, pomegranate, ginger — the early blossom like snow—and many flowering shrubs. The house was a picturesque ruin. Golden carp of a tremendous size swam lazily around the pool in the sun and a flock of pigeons periodically left the earth for a flight into the blue.[22]

As the years went by, McBey began, as Monet had done at Giverny, to concentrate on painting his garden and the spectacular views from its leafy shelter. On one occasion, he painted a panorama of the garden with the sea in the background (this painting was recently donated to Aberdeen Art Gallery). Most years he would complete several watercolours, either of the views from Jalobey or from the Cherifian Rocks nearby.

Plate 29 *The Straits of Gibraltar from Cherifian Rocks* 1948 pen, ink & watercolour.

Plate 30 *Tangier — A View over the Bay* 1956 pen, ink & watercolour.

McBey also set about restoring the house and adding a studio. In spite of the primitive living conditions—Jalobey had no telephone, electricity and only the simplest of cooking arrangements—the McBeys entertained there and their friends came to love the place as much as they did. Marguerite's mother came too, eventually buying a house a little further down the hill.

Whilst Jalobey was being renovated the McBeys rented a house nearby. A Moroccan who worked there was to become a great friend. A young man from the Atlas Mountains, Scouri had a wonderful sense of humour which appealed greatly to McBey, who was himself a great joker and raconteur. He would entertain McBey constantly with his jokes and anecdotes, usually concerning his fishing; Scouri used to fish, as men still do today, from the rocks at Cap Spartel, just a little way along the coast from Jalobey.

Plate 31 *Panoramic View from Jalobey* pen, ink & watercolour.

Life in Morocco settled down to long days of painting, working on the house, talking to the locals, drinking mint tea and delighting in Scouri's latest exploit. Scouri may have had something to do with the choice of a donkey for McBey's fiftieth birthday present, a gift which was to delight its new owner:

He seemed so weak and thin-legged that I hesitated to ride him far, so I asked our Arab gardener how much I could use him. He asked how much I weighed. I got paper and calculated from stones to pounds, from pounds to kilos. When he got this he took the paper and went into a huddle with the other Arab who did his work. They calculated and disputed for three quarters of an hour, then came to the verdict, 'Señor, you can sit on him for photo, but not ride him'.[23]

The donkey was called Hadji (an honorary title meaning 'traveller' allowed to those who have made the sacred pilgrimage to Mecca). Hadji accounted for the purchase of a great deal of grain over the years but did very little work, Shaib, the gardener, preferring his sister-in-law to carry any heavy loads.

Plate 32 James McBey seated on Hadji, circa 1933.

Plate 33 *Scouri Looking out to Sea* pen, ink & watercolour.

Plate 34 *Hortense Loeb on a swing at The Gazebo* 1936 pen, ink & watercolour.

In Morocco, country women traditionally do much of the heavy lifting, a reversal of roles which rather horrified some of McBey's American friends. He found their reaction amusing, and would counteract their protestations by saying: 'Have you ever noticed the expression on the faces of these country women — beasts of burden? They look happy and are sometimes even singing. Now, when you go back study the faces of the women on 57th street or in the elevators of Saks 5th Avenue. They look so unhappy and worried as to where they are going to buy their new hat'.[24]

McBey delighted in the Moroccan country people's lack of sophistication and what he felt to be their correct sense of priorities. Writing to a friend during the Second World War he remembered his feeling of wellbeing during his many sojourns in Morocco: 'The feeling you describe you have — not being worried about anything — is truly very pleasant. I have never been able to rise to it in Scotland or England or America, but I do get it in Tangier without any effort. It is the state of mind we ought to have, but in the very civilized and sophisticated countries it is smothered by layers of responsibilities'.[25]

From Jalobey, McBey would go down to the twice-weekly markets held in the Soko in Tangier. Here the country women from the Riff mountains would gather to sell fruit, vegetables, cheese and chickens. Their traditional costume — which is still worn today — delighted McBey and he was to paint these colourfully clad women again and again.

The principal element of the costume is the *foutra*, a rectangle of white cotton, striped red or blue. This the Riffian women wrap round their hips, and another they tuck under their hat. The hat is huge and made of straw. It is decorated with enormous red or blue pompons and cords. Under all these thick clothes they look very bulky, but unlike some of the city women, they do not cover their faces, and their exquisite olive-skinned complexions, large brown eyes and sparkling teeth stay clearly visible.

The simple beauty of the Riffian women appealed greatly to McBey. He painted the portraits of some, exalting their simplicity and unaffected ways in a magnificent series of portraits. Normally, he would paint in oils, as he did in watercolour, using washes of pure colour. In his *Anjera Peasant Girl*, for example, McBey draws the image in black, then fills in using broad strokes of brilliant colour, a painting method which owes no small debt to Cezanne, whose landscapes and still-life pictures (though not, interestingly, his portraits) were by the 1930s proving to be a great influence on the otherwise artistically isolated McBey.

Plates 35, 36 & 37   Riffian Women at the Market in Tangier 1989.

Plate 38 *Anjera Peasant Girl* 1936 oil on canvas.

Plate 39 *Peasant Girl* 1936 oil on canvas.

As well as single portraits, McBey continued to make quick pen-and-ink sketches: groups of figures gathered to bargain over their wares in the market, or sheltering from the strong sun in small shops set into the walls of the city. In all these sketches, McBey manages to suggest bodily form under the heavy robes worn by the country people and each study is full of lively action. One senses the noise and movement of these Thursday and Sunday markets which are still a colouristic delight, not to be missed if visiting Tangier.

Sometimes McBey would travel a little further along the coast to paint the Riffians coming into town. On the Malabata Road (today lined with large hotels, but in McBey's day with eucalyptus trees) and the beach below, the women would trundle, their wares wrapped up in a large *foutra* on their backs.

Every Thursday I have been out stalking the charcoal women coming in from the Riff, along the eucalyptus avenue and have made four or five watercolour drawings. In some of these I have managed to capture some of the excited atmosphere that accompanies the figures. I'm trying in these watercolour drawings to convey a definite atmosphere with as great an economy of means as possible, which implies a spontaneity of technique admitting of no alteration.[26]

Plate 40 *Flower Market in The Soko Grande, Tangier* circa 1946 pen, ink & watercolour.

The materials which McBey used for these watercolours were the finest available. Since his first visit to the Netherlands in 1910 he had collected old paper. He liked the way this old paper had become, as he described it, 'friendly' with age: 'the skin of old paper has become soft and velvety, due to the action of time on the surface size, while the strength of the actual paper has not been impaired'.[27]

For ink McBey had tried to find an old formula, but found that he could achieve a rich brown by mixing brown and black Quink. In London he had found at Windsor Newton a supply of eighteenth-century pencils, the Cumberland lead encased in cedar wood and, having found what he believed to be the perfect pencil, he had bought the complete stock. In Morocco, he collected rainwater for his watercolours, so as to make sure that it was as clean and pure as possible.

His technique of watercolour painting was enhanced by his perfectionism and attention to such details. As the years passed, his paintings began to take on an almost Japanese simplicity, line being the most important element, but enhanced with soft watercolour washes, mauves (for the shadows), pale blue, terracotta, yellow and olive green.

Plate 41 *Vegetable Market, Tangier* pen, ink & watercolour.

Plate 42 *Tangier Beach* 1948 pen, ink & watercolour.

Plate 43 *Malabata Road, Tangier* 1958 pen, ink & watercolour.

Plate 44 *Countrywoman Selling Oranges, Tangier* 1935 pen, ink & watercolour.

Plate 45 *Figure Studies, Tangier Beach* 1948 pen, ink & watercolour.

In January and February, when rain in Tangier was the norm, the McBeys would travel the 500 kilometres to Marrakesh where, in 1937 they had purchased a small house in the Medina. Like Jalobey, the house was delapidated, but McBey set about the task of restoring it with great enthusiasm. Once again the exploits of the wily Moroccan workmen were a source of constant amusement, and tales of the repair work were to become McBey's favourite repertoire. One Friday the head mason took out his watch, studied it lengthily and asked McBey if he could have the afternoon off:

'Do you expect to be paid for the time?', McBey asked.

'Yes, indeed', he replied.

'Well, then, I think I am entitled to know where you are going.'

Without a moment's reflection, he replied, 'Monsieur, I am going to the mosque to thank Allah for sending you here'.[28]

In spite of domestic difficulties, James McBey's artistic output was prodigious. He would wander the narrow streets of Marrakesh with a young man in tow to keep the younger children away, delighting in the myriad sounds and sights of this hot, southern city. On one of the many trips to the Souks to find carpets and furniture for the house, he came across the Silk Souk, where silk cloth and thread would be dyed in the morning and hung up to dry in the afternoon. McBey was hypnotised by the spectactle and immediately set about painting the scene, first in watercolour and, when he returned home, in oil. On either side of a massive Islamic arch swathes of cloth are hanging up to dry. In the watercolour sketch, the viewpoint is rather low, and most of the rush roof of the market is visible. In the oil painting, McBey moved slightly to the right and heightened his viewpoint so that the arch in the background

Plate 46 *The Silk Souk, Marrakesh* 1936 pen, ink & watercolour.

becomes centred and a focal point in the picture. Instead of the small gathering of people present when McBey first sketched the Souk, he depicts a huge crowd which has gathered to bargain over the silk. Only the seated man who rests his head on his hand to the left remains in the final painting. All the other figures are added anew, with bold characterisations, such as the enormously fat man in the centre of the canvas and his companion in a boldly striped *djellaba*. The subtle shades of the silk — terracotta, pink, blue, yellow and green — are echoed in the brightly coloured clothes of the crowd, the final composition being a tour-de-force of colour and movement.

Frequently, McBey would go outside the city to paint the famous red walls of Marrakesh. In 1938 he completed an etching of the scene. *Outside the Walls, Marrakesh* is a simple composition formed by a series of diagonals — the city walls to the right and palm trees to the left. Turning increasingly to watercolour painting, McBey's etchings became fewer and fewer. His last Moroccan etching, and arguably the finest, *Marrakesh*, surveys the huge vista of the Djema el F'naa, the main market place of Marrakesh.

Plate 47 *The Silk Souk, Marrakesh* 1936 oil on canvas.

Community life in Marrakesh centres upon the large open space of the Djema el F'naa which, roughly translated, means 'the meeting place of the dead' or 'the sinner's rendezvous' since it was there that, until the arrival of the French, the heads and limbs of executed criminals were exposed to public view. By the 1930s, the Djema el F'naa had become entirely a meeting place of the living; a central meeting point for both trade and amusement with farmers, Berbers from the mountains and the men of distant tribes beyond the Atlas Mountains gathering to bargain, buy and sell. To cater for them an assortment of townspeople would trade in the square too: soup vendors, orange sellers, clothes merchants, women

Plate 48   The Silk Souk, Fès 1989.

selling bread and vegetables, even dentists pulling teeth in the open air and barbers shaving and bleeding the country people. Moroccan superstitions were also well catered for by the sellers of charms against the *Djinn* (evil spirits) and other magical potions. Indeed, the market place became a sort of open-air theatre where snake charmers, acrobats, story-tellers and musicians would gather, accompanied by the monotonous but hypnotizing rhythm of cymbals, tambourines and drums.

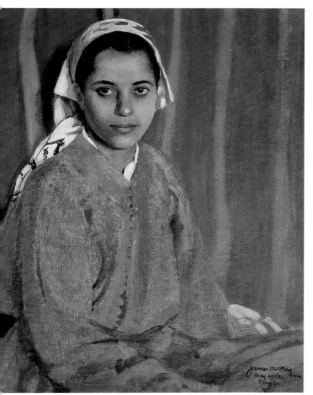

The bustle, noise and varicoloured garb of the crowd made McBey's eyes 'stand out like organ stops',[29] and he realised the Djema el F'naa to be the perfect subject for a painting. Then, as now, however, the Moroccan people did not like to be depicted. However, he managed to persuade a little acrobat boy and his five-year-old sister, Zorah, to go back to his house in the Medina and sit for him. It was in November 1936 that the two began to sit. They obviously enjoyed their new employment and soon all three became good friends. In spite of it being a studio picture, *Acrobats, Marrakesh* captures the action and bustle of that remarkable market place. McBey's brave use of bold colours and his ability to depict an expectant crowd whose every gesture suggests tension, excitement and enjoyment increases the forcefulness of the image. T⁺ child-like pose of Zorah, who seems ͻomewhat dazzled by all the attention, is contrasted with that of her older brother who, seated in the foreground, appears much more confident.

Plate 49   *Zorah* 1952 oil on canvas.

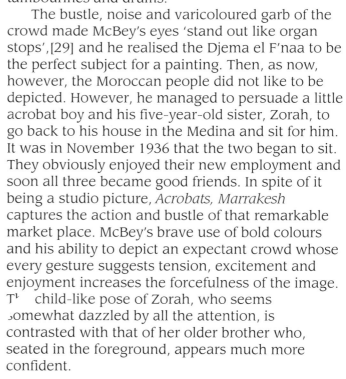

59

Plate 50 *Acrobats, Marrakesh* 1936 oil on canvas.

Plate 51 *Marrakesh* 1938 etching.

Plate 52 *Marrakesh* 1933 pen, ink & watercolour.
Plate 53 *Gateway, Marrakesh* 1933 pen, ink & watercolour.

Plate 54 *Courtyard, Marrakesh* 1933 pen, ink & watercolour.
Plate 55 *Mosque, Marrakesh* 1933 pen, ink & watercolour.

Plate 56 *City Walls, Marrakesh* 1950 pen, ink & watercolour.
Plate 57 *Outside the Walls, Marrakesh* 1938 etching.

Plate 58 A market stall, Fès 1989.

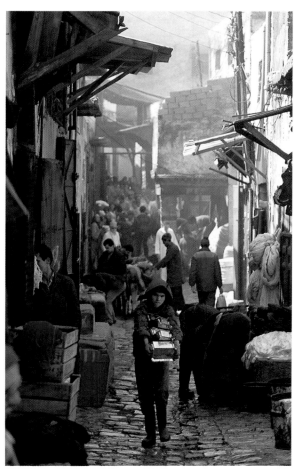

Plate 59 The Silk Souk, Fès 1989.

Throughout the early thirties, in his house in the Marrakesh Medina, McBey continued to paint portraits, though his subject matter was proving to be more colourful than it had been in Britain. Instead of company directors and bank managers, he painted the glittering prostitutes of the city. In one of the finest of these portraits, he depicts one of the women as a sort of goddess. Seated full face, cross legged, she wears a magnificent white and gold dress. McBey, who collected fine old frames, put this painting in a gold Florentine frame, the marbling on which matches perfectly the colours in the painting. Painting and frame are as one — a total unified work of art. In another study of a prostitute, similar colour combinations are employed: the pinks, gold and white of the woman's headress and robe are echoed in the striped cloth draped over the bed on which she reclines. The haughty look of this heavily made-up prostitute is in total contrast to the peasant women of McBey's Tangier sojourns, and indeed all the Marrakesh pictures have a rather more exotic feel.

Plate 60 *Prostitute in White and Gold* oil on canvas.

Plate 61 *Prostitute* circa 1938 oil on canvas.

The colourful characters of this Bohemian city became the McBeys' friends and one such, a woman known to everyone simply as Odette, sat for McBey in about 1937. The portrait which resulted is as sensual as any he ever painted and manages to convey all the mystique and exotic qualities associated with Arab culture. Odette had been a dancer in the Djema el F'naa but had gone to France as a young woman and returned to Morocco with short hair, European clothes and a French name. She then proceeded to shock the Moroccan community by opening a chic restaurant, where the resident Europeans could dine on Moroccan specialities. When working at her restaurant, she would dress in traditional costume, and it was thus that McBey chose to depict her. She stares out of the canvas defiantly, a dark and mysterious face, framed by a thick, dark wood frame selected by McBey to increase the mystery of the sitter. McBey's contemporary portraits of the Europeans living in Morocco, such as the fine study of Clemence Bonnet Mathews, were often just as exotic, with oriental still life detail and rich terracotta the primary colour.

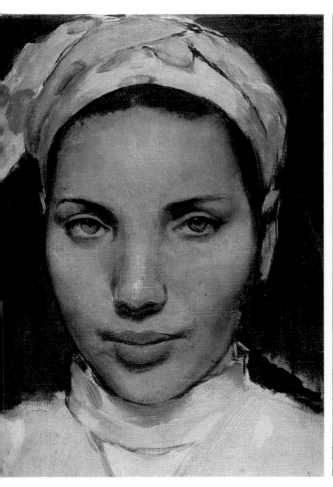

Plate 62 *Odette* circa 1937 oil on canvas.

Plate 63 Clemence Bonnet Mathews 1937 oil on canvas.

67

From Marrakesh the snow-capped peaks of the Atlas Mountains are clearly visible to the south. It was in 1936 that McBey decided to cross these high mountains with his friend Lord Rowallan.[30] Some of McBey's finest landscape paintings resulted from this journey, which took Rowallan, Marguerite and James McBey through the Tizi-n-Tichka Pass, one of the three traditional routes south over the Atlas Mountains. The huge mountains rise majestically from vast flat plains. Lying roughly in the middle of the Atlas Mountains, Tizi-n-Tichka Pass was the main communication route connecting Marrakesh with the large land basin to the south and, at 2260 metres, was the highest pass with a road in Morocco. McBey could not let such a superb view go unrecorded. Once again, he worked from sketches, finishing the oil in the studio. Broad shapes and flat expanses of colour, strong diagonals sliced through the composition, snow covered peaks in the background juxtaposed with a dark, forbidding foreground combine to give a dramatic impression of the height and magnificence of the pass.

They travelled in great style, in a 1923 Rolls Royce Silver Ghost which McBey had bought in Wimbledon several years previously. In his autobiography Rowallan remembered the trip with fondness:

The Rolls was piled with provisions and bedding, for there were no air-conditioned hotels with restaurants and private bathrooms for weary travellers. Our bed was what we could make it, in a wayside pension, our food that of the country. How good the mint tea was, and the couscous. The journey was not without an element of danger and one had to inform the Foreign Legion of one's itinerary, in case of a 'wrong turning'.[31]

Plate 64 *The Atlas Mountains* 1950 pen, ink & watercolour.

Plate 65 *The Atlas Mountains* 1938 etching.

McBey, who had been brought up on the flat lands of the Ythan estuary, was not used to such high mountains; he was too frightened to drive on this precipitous road, and would not trust anyone else's driving either. So Rowallan drove and McBey walked over the highest and steepest part of the journey. Fortunately, there were no mishaps and the three crossed the pass and descended to Ouarzazate, a mud village dominated by a great kasbah on the River Draa.

In 1939, McBey returned to Britain and, like many people during that long, hot summer, his thoughts were far from the possibility of imminent war. Writing to Marguerite's mother on 27 August, he gives no hint of how life was to change: 'Marguerite arrived safely on Friday night amid a terrific crowd of returning holiday people from the Continent, the train came in six portions. She was four hours late.'[32]. Even once war was declared, he remained optimistic and evidently hoped to return to his beloved Morocco soon:

When I saw you off that day at Victoria I did not think there would be war so soon. I saw by your letter to Marguerite that you had a very wonderful landing at Tangier. I do hope that the war will not affect you out there. I don't see why it should as Spain is now at peace internally and is to remain neutral in the present war, as is Italy. I see also the Italian liners are sailing to New York as usual, so you will not feel you cannot get away if you want to ... sailing permits are now required for anyone going abroad, and regulations etc change from day to day, but in a little Marguerite and I will try to get to Tangier.[33]

Plate 66 *The Atlas Mountains* circa 1938 oil on canvas.

Plate 67 *The Tizi-n-Tichka Pass* 1936 oil on canvas.

with all good wishes from
James McBey
marguerite McBey

Plate 68 *Sketch for a Christmas Card* pen & ink.

It was not to be. As the war intensified, American citizens were told that they could not have their safety guaranteed abroad. Marguerite had to return to the United States and McBey, fearing they might therefore be parted for several years, decided to accompany her. On arrival Marguerite's passport was taken by the Immigration authorities and McBey, at the age of fifty six, found himself uprooted, without access to his assets, and virtually penniless. Forced to make a new career he rented a studio in New York, where he worked on several portrait commissions. On visits to Marguerite's mother in Philadelphia, McBey made many watercolours of the surrounding countryside. Marguerite's brother had given them a small car and in this they travelled through Maryland and Virginia to North Carolina. After several months of touring around, staying with relatives and feeling, as McBey put it,'like refugees', they returned to New York where McBey continued to paint portraits, though the staple diet was, once again, the rather dull fodder of managing directors and members of the board. In New York their social life was hectic and, though McBey loved to entertain, sometimes it all became too much. His thoughts remained with the country he had now come to regard as home: 'We have wandered over about half the States here in the last five years and every spot we came to which gave the impression God had lingered there we instinctively compared it with Tangier … But, for myself give me Tangier!'.[34] He constantly yearned to return to Morocco and, knowing this was impossible, he became more and more depressed: 'It will be too hot for Marrakesh, but in my imagination Tangier spells heaven. Here you feel you are caught in the middle of an endless jazz floor and if you don't jazz too you will get trampled under'.[35]

In the spring of 1941 the McBeys travelled to California, as McBey had always wanted to see the West. In early November, they reached San Francisco. McBey loved the city and managed to rent a flat on Russian Hill, which overlooks the Bay, much as Jalobey did the Straits of Gibraltar. The West appealed to McBey, but the similarities to Morocco merely increased his longing to return there: 'Los Angeles is exactly like Tangier, minus the Arabs, but it is sixty miles from one end to the other. The eucalyptus, mimosa and oleander gave us a nasty dose of nostalgia.[36]

He drew comparisons constantly: 'The weather has now turned delightful — real Tangier weather, a blue sky and a hot sun and a fresh cool air'.[37]

In 1942 McBey had rented a studio apartment at 11 Macdougal Alley, a little cul-de-sac in Greenwich Village, just at the beginning of 5th Avenue. The McBeys lived there almost continuously until the end of the war and kept the house on until 1952, McBey returning there occasionally to complete portrait commissions.

McBey, by now an elderly man, was unable to adapt to his new surroundings. Indeed he seemed to stick more doggedly to the traditions of his youth. Ever present were his long-held beliefs to which he clung obsessively, as if they were the one tenuous link with his past life in Scotland. Remembering the Sabbath of his youth, for example, McBey never knowingly worked·on Sundays. On one occasion when he did, by accident, work past midnight on Saturday, he felt it necessary to record the misdemeanour in his diary: 'Worked till 12.30. Hope God will give me a special dispensation for half an hour on Sunday'.[38]

Plate 69 James McBey

By March 1944 McBey had become deeply depressed by the whole situation: 'James is very restless and seems unhappy. He sits for hours reading newspapers.'[39] He found the summer heat of New York very trying and it only increased his dissatisfaction with his situation: 'These continual heat waves are turning my body to butter and I want to go to the edge of the Atlantic somewhere so that it may get a chance to solidify again'.[40]

In his worst moments, he despaired of ever returning to Morocco but took some consolation in his memories of his time there: 'I thank Heaven often for the memories I possess of Morocco ... As we get older we dwell more and more on the past like cows chewing the cud and those of us who have a good stomach full of memories are to be counted lucky. Because of this I grudge the years eaten by the Bank and the Nazis.'[41] As soon as peace was declared McBey began to prepare for his return to Morocco. For the first time McBey flew; on 8 May 1946 Marguerite and he took a TWA flight to Lisbon. After several frustrating days wait in Portugal which he filled painting some fine watercolours of the city, McBey finally set off for Tangier.

His relief on returning to Morocco is revealed in his diary entry for the 15th May, his first day back, and even the destruction of many of his precious possessions could not quell his excitement: 'M & I walked to Socco Chico by full moon — it is good to be back again. THANK YOU GOD. Lots to be done mirrors broken beloved telescope in pieces. Jalobey completely overgrown.'[42] Soon he was busy putting the house back into order:

FIRST NIGHT SPENT AT JALOBEY — beautiful with clouds. Got lamps from Arab all fixed more or less. Got suitcases and off to Jalobey, M holding lamps on her knees. Ali and Dris cutting trees — masons repairing brick pergola — Shaib planting marguerites. Strange how fascinating it is to watch the Arabs work. Night fell gradually — very calm — nothing but dull hum of sea — very dark — very bright stars — occasionally the croaking of a frog. This is what I have thought of so often for seven long years. I am so glad that it is granted to me to be here again. God I thank you.[43]

The following year James McBey did little painting, for he was fully occupied writing his autobiography. The book covered his early life: his harsh upbringing, his years working at the detested Bank and his early artistic career. McBey had great reservations about his literary skills but the story, simply told, remains a bravely honest account of a lifestyle now long gone. Running throughout the book is McBey's sense of humour, his love of jokes and pranks, his fears and insecurities, his Scottish straightforwardness and honesty. Also present is a driving ambition fuelled by an inborn love of art and strong wish to paint and etch.

For McBey, Morocco acted as a catharsis: after years of travelling, trying to prove himself as a man and an artist, he was at last at peace with the world. He put this down to the lifestyle in Tangier and was always trying to encourage his friends to try the treatment: 'I am sure Tangier would relax you and give you a clearer slant on life, and I know of no place which, taken all in all, has so much of what all of us, at bottom, hanker after'.[44]

It was in 1948 that McBey realised a long wished dream. He negotiated the successful purchase of the house he had stayed in on his first visit to Tangier in 1913. El Foolk lay just a little way up the Old Mountain from Jalobey. It was a simple, unpretentious house with a sturdy simplicity that appealed to McBey (it had once been a stable). One gable end stood like the prow of a ship into the rising sun and its name, which translated meant 'The Ark', was an appropriate one. Higher than Jalobey, it commanded a superb view over the Straits of

Gibraltar. There was no studio, however, and the house was too small for the McBeys, so once more, McBey became involved in building repairs and alterations, this time on a massive scale. He knew what he wanted and kept a close eye on the workmen to see that the house was renovated and enlarged in the traditional manner. The Arabs' idiosyncratic ways of working intrigued and amused McBey and he began to keep a visual account of the progress on the house. A notebook always at hand, he would visit the site most days to record the latest improvement, problem, conversation, price or payment.

Plate 70 *El Foolk* circa 1947 pen, ink & watercolour.

Left: Plate 71 El Foolk 1989.

Plate 72

Plate 74

Plate 73

Plate 72 *Reconstruction of El Foolk — Building the East wall* 1949 pen, ink & watercolour: Friday 5th August 1949: At the garage the wire had been laid over the roof and they are mixing cement and stones by hand and laying it all over, packing it down with a stick. Above they are building above the 1.20 metre line and are building between the windows and doors.
Now the passage doors have been burst into the S. of the hall there is a through draft making it very cool.
At 5 p.m. they finished the ceiling of the garage by spreading grout over it.
Above the E. wall they have gone up 5 feet from the window sill, elsewhere about 3 feet.
Made two drawings.

Plate 73 *Reconstruction of El Foolk — Carrying bricks and Plaster* 1949 pen, ink & watercolour: Monday 5th September 1949: Paco went on roof and placed bricks for parapet whilst I went down to road and shouted up to M who translated to him how far in to come. Decided parapet should come in 5 cm. Carpenter is nailing laith to middle N. room having finished N.E. room. Tonio is plastering ceiling of E. half of new bedrooms.

Plate 74 *Reconstruction of El Foolk — The Tree Men* 1949 pen, ink & watercolour: Monday 19th September 1949: The two tree men turned up, but one was ill and went home. The other Ali worked at cutting the branches of eucalyptus to the S. They got quite a lot off by noon but the stalk of the tree still stands.

One day Framit, the Spanish paymaster, arrived holding a piece of dark wood, as heavy as iron. He regretted the high quote he had had to give for oak, and wondered if McBey would mind accepting this dark wood instead. McBey immediately recognised it to be teak, and bought not only enough to floor the entire house, but the whole consignment. With the left over pieces he had large, heavy pieces of furniture made in the Spanish manner, a style he had admired for many years. On New Year's Eve 1949, the McBeys moved in. McBey became completely absorbed with the renovations of the house and the furnishing of it.

His Heath Robinson-ish approach to decor was described in many letters. In one, he relates his delight at the latest acquisition, a 36-inch reflector from some giant war-time searchlight:

> I got sent out from England a 3 feet(!) convex mirror which with the aid of the Mackay radio carpenter we have put above the fireplace, hiding the recess. Everybody's eyes are on the mirror, no matter who they are talking to. It is really funny.[45]

Plate 75 The Sitting Room, El Foolk.

McBey began to have masses of earth in the garden moved, to form a series of terraces and eating areas. When the alterations to the house were complete, a Kufic device was hoisted into the east wall under the eaves. It read 'I have entrusted myself to God'. Though McBey had forsaken traditional religion at an early age, he continued to believe in God and to pray when he wanted something very badly.

He also had a Presbyterian view of hard work, believing that his good fortune should be repaid with work. An excursion to the beach to lie in the sun or swim was always turned by McBey into an expedition to collect pebbles for the garden paths. He could have had a life of leisure but had a strong belief that 'Hard Is Good'. Equally he was a prodigious artist. Above his bed at El Foolk he had hung Sir Jacob Astley's famous prayer written before the Battle of Newbury during the English Civil War:

> LORD
> I shall be very busy this day
> I may forget Thee
> but do not Thou forget me.

Indeed he was busy every day, a discipline made easier by his tendency to wake early. 'He would wake very early and with impatience would await the rising of the sun. As long as I knew him he woke each morning new and refreshed and bright-eyed like a child — eager for the adventure each day would bring'.[46]

A small viewing tower was added to the top of the house and from there McBey could scan the bay. A room at the top of the tower contained his telescopes, as well as early charts and maps of the region and his own drawing of the sunrise, an ink sketch measuring $6\frac{1}{2}$ x 26 inches depicting a 45° panorama of the view across the water. Every few months between 1952 and 1959 McBey would note the position of the rising sun and fill it in on the drawing.

Plate 76 The Telescope Room, El Foolk.

Using his very powerful telescope (a Zeiss telescope of 100 magnifications) he could spy passengers and cargo on ships, and even see cars in Gibraltar, thirty-eight miles away, or watch boys playing football in Tarifa in Spain. His delight with the telescope was like that of a boy: 'Wheeled my big telescope out on roof terrace. Cool, big clouds and still. Visibility amazing. Watched old three masted boat trying to make Tangier. Saw three cars of people at bottom of tower in Spain. Saw the church spire at Medina Sidonia (49 miles away). Glad I got a telescope'.[47]

McBey delighted in his voyeuristic abilities. As an artist he had always wanted to sketch people without their knowing. From his earliest days in Morocco this had proved almost impossible; due to his features and physique, he stood out in a crowd. The telescope overcame this problem: he could become the unseen companion of the passing ships. McBey was fascinated by the sea and with man's relation to it. The telescope allowed him to scan the seascape around the house, and to paint it in comfort and seclusion. Sometimes, however, he visited the long beach to the east of Tangier to sketch the fishermen hauling in their nets as they still do today.

McBey continued to paint portraits, amongst them a fine self-portrait and one of Marguerite seated in the garden of El Foolk. The portraits, which form a pair, show both sitters in a confident, relaxed pose. Marguerite, in simple clothes, has just finished a meal and is relaxing in one of the dining areas of the garden. McBey's eye for colour would overrule what the sitter wanted to wear — portraying his wife in casual, unsophisticated clothes was typical. One young girl was reduced to tears after she was forbidden by McBey to wear either of the two Dior dresses she had brought for her sitting. Instead McBey insisted on her wearing a simple cotton dress.

Plate 77 *Tangier Port* 1951 pen, ink & watercolour.

Plate 78 *Bringing in the Nets, Tangier Port* 1951 pen, ink & watercolour.

James McBey   Tangier July 1951.

Plate 79 *Tangier: On the Beach* 1953 pen, ink & watercolour.

Plate 80 Tangier Beach 1989.

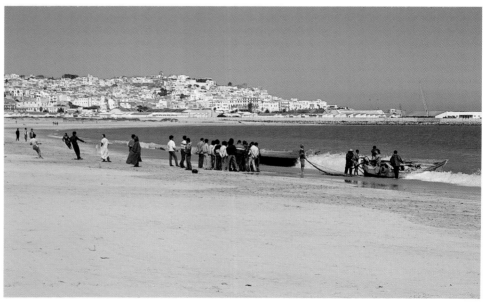

To live in Morocco was, for McBey, the ideal. Though he returned often to Scotland —
even in his last year — it always saddened him. Morocco had the same broad expanses of
land, sea and sky which he recognised from Scotland, but all bathed in warm sunshine. 'The
days glide past so quietly here that when the Arab maid's wages fall due at the end of the
month it comes as a surprise ... The weather is heavenly here just now. Cloudless skies, a hot
sun and cool wind, a silent radio. I sit often and wonder what I have done to deserve this
peace and no newspapers'.[48]

In 1959 McBey had a hectic time, travelling to Philadelphia, Miami, Trinidad, Grenada,
Antigua, Aberdeen, London, Gibraltar and back to Tangier. On 3 March he had visited his
mother's grave at East Pitscalf, Mains of Foveran, near Newburgh.

In November he contracted pneumonia. He tried to fight it off, as he had always done, by
working, cutting logs. He became seriously ill and on 1 December, he died. McBey had had, by
any standards, a long and successful life. As he saw it, luck had followed him throughout.
Starting in a harsh, unloving world he had been privileged to end it fulfilled and content. Many
years before, a good friend had summed up in a poem this uncanny luck that McBey believed
in so strongly:

> The wonder grows from day to day
> How God can look after James McBey
> When, as the Bible says he oughter
> He casts his bread upon the water
> Lo! It returns upon the tide
> well buttered on the other side.
> When servants leave him, is he stranded?
> No. God is much too open handed —
> He takes two angels from the Host
> and sends them via The Morning Post
> No wonder France is still in debt
> and baulked the Balkans fume and fret,
> And trade is in a dreadful plight —
> God has no time to put things right:
> He's far too busy, night and day,
> In doing things for James McBey.[49]

It was, perhaps, simply modesty that allowed McBey to believe that so many of his
achievements in life had been arrived at through luck alone. In fact, James McBey escaped
from his past through a combination of many remarkable personal qualities. He achieved
artistic success not merely through luck, but by extreme hard work, driving ambition and an
innate talent which he had the intelligence to develop with little, if any, outside
encouragement or training. His personal life was tempestuous at times, reflecting his own
highly emotional character and understandable insecurities brought about by a difficult
childhood. In spite of this, McBey was loved and admired by the people around him. He had a
remarkable sense of humour — though his practical jokes could be cruelly cutting at times —

and he was a superb raconteur. His interest in others and enjoyment of good company meant that he was never short of friends and when he died he was sorely missed by many. One passage from a letter to his wife, written soon after McBey's death, sums up the feelings he could bring about in his companions: 'I shall always remember him and his laugh, and his canny cautiousness and eagerness to avoid being taken for a ride'.[50] In most of the letters written to Marguerite McBey at this time there is obviously a sadness at the passing of a life but a happiness too in having been privileged to know this remarkable man.

McBey was buried on his own land, Cherifian rocks. The simple grave looks out to sea — the view he knew so well and painted so often. Inscribed on the headstone with his name and dates is a short but significant phrase, written in Arabic: 'He Loved Morocco'.

Plate 81 James McBey at work, El Foolk.

Plate 82 *Marguerite McBey* 1950 oil on canvas.

Plate 83 *Self Portrait* 1952 oil on canvas.

After McBey's death, Marguerite McBey donated a vast collection of his paintings, prints, drawings and memorabilia to Aberdeen Art Gallery. She also provided the money to build a print room where the collection could be housed and displayed. Some years later, Aberdeen's holding of McBey's work was further enhanced when a good friend of McBey, Harold H. Kynett, bequeathed his entire collection to The University of Aberdeen. It seems that Kynett thought that the Art Gallery belonged to The University, but this mistake has been rectified by the most generous permanent loan of all the items in The Kynett Bequest to The Art Gallery. As recently as 1988, Mrs McBey further enhanced the collections of Aberdeen Art Gallery with the donation of her husband's letters, diaries, scrapbooks and photographs. In the United States, Boston Public Library received in 1941 the collection of McBey's work once owned by the one-time President of The Chase Bank, Albert H. Wiggin. The National Gallery in Washington acquired the collection owned by Lessing Rosenwald. McBey's war work (including an oil portrait of Lawrence of Arabia) is housed largely in The Imperial War Museum and The British Museum, London whilst in Tangier, The Old American Legation has a fine display of his oil paintings, prints and drawings. The entire output of such a hard-working artist as McBey, however, could never be contained in three or four large collections and hundreds of his prints and paintings remain in the hands of numerous private collectors. Indeed, he was such a prolific artist that it is still possible to pick up his work at a country sale or small gallery. His style is immediately recognisable and his swift, lively pen strokes and an unmistakable vivacity and freedom of handling continue to emanate from that fine 'friendly' paper, some forty, fifty or sixty years after the work's creation.

Plate 84 Dining Room of the Old American Legation, Tangier 1989.

Notes

1. McBey, James 'An Artist's Wanderings', *The Graphic*, 14 January 1922
2. The book was Maxime Lalanne's *A Treatise on Etching*, translated from the French by S.R. Koehler. McBey put so much store in the effect this book had on his career, that many years later he presented Aberdeen Public Library with a new copy of the book and was permitted to retain the original copy for his own library. This book is now in the collections of Aberdeen Art Gallery.
3. McBey, James *The Early Life of James McBey*, Ed. Nicholas Barker, OUP, 1977, p. 103.
4. cf. *James Kerr Lawson — A Canadian Abroad*, Art Gallery of Windsor, Ontario, 1983
5. Hardie, Martin *Etchings & Dry Points from 1902 to 1924 by James McBey*, P & D Colnaghi & Co., 1925, p. xii
6. Letter to Mr and Mrs Bryce, 1912
7. 'An Aberdeen Artist's Adventures — Mr McBey's Moroccan Tour' (by our London Correspondent), *Aberdeen Press & Journal*, 18 March 1913
8. McBey, James 'An Artist's Wanderings', *The Graphic*, 14 January 1922, p. 14.
9. Ibid. p. 14.
10. G. P. Chalmers' *The Legend* was acquired by The National Gallery of Scotland in 1905. It was etched by Paul Rajon for the Royal Association and there seems no doubt that McBey would have seen either the painting or the etching before 1912.
11. Salaman, Malcolm C. 'The Etchings of James McBey', *Studio*, 1913, Vol. 58, pp. 32–34 (published February 1913)
12. See note 3, p. 114
13. See note 7
14. Ibid.
15. See note 8
16. Ibid.
17. See note 7
18. Memoirs of Marguerite McBey (unpublished)
19. Ibid.
20. Ibid.
21. Ibid.
22. Ibid.
23. Letter to W. Logan MacCoy, 19 June 1945
24. See note 18
25. Letter to Herbert Paton, 28 February 1944
26. Letter to Maurice J. Strauss, 3 October 1958
27. See note 5
28. See note 18
29. Ibid.
30. Sir Thomas Godfrey Polson Corbett of Rowallan was born on 19 December 1895. He is today best remembered in his role of Chief Scout of the British Commonwealth, a post he held from 1945. Rowallan commissioned McBey to paint a portrait of each of his eight children when they became twelve years old; he also painted Rowallan in the uniform of Chief Scout.

31. *Rowallan — An autobiography*, Paul Harris, 1976, p. 59
32. Letter to Hortense Loeb, 27 August 1939
33. Ibid. 8 September 1939
34. Letter to Dr William Murray, 24 January 1945
35. See note 31
36. Letter to Herbert Paton, 26 November 1941
37. Ibid. 22 September 1941
38. Diary of James McBey, Saturday, 4 November 1941
39. Diary of Marguerite McBey, March 1944
40. Letter to H.H. Kynett, 15 July 1943
41. Letter to Lord Rowallan, 24 August 1944
42. Diary of James McBey, 15 May 1946
43. Ibid. 27 May 1946
44. Letter to Herbert Paton, 18 January 1947
45. Letter to Lisbeth, 26 December 1951
46. See note 18
47. Diary of James McBey, 13 April 1952
48. Letter to H.H. Kynett, 28 October 1953
49. Poem written by E. Arnott Robinson ('Billy'), author of *Callum*. See note 18
50. Letter from Harold Wright to Marguerite McBey, 1959

Illustration Acknowledgements

Aberdeen City Arts Department, Art Gallery & Museums
1, 5, 6, 7, 8, 10, 11, 12, 13, 14, 15, 16, 17, 19, 23, 28, 31, 42, 51, 52, 57, 65, 66, 77, 78.

Old American Collection, Tangier
3, 9, 29, 40, 49, 60, 64.

Mike Davidson
2, 4, 20, 21, 22, 27, 35, 36, 37, 48, 58, 59, 71, 75, 76, 80, 84, back cover.

Malcolm Forbes
18, 30, 41, 43, 53, 54, 79.

Clemence Bonnet Mathews
63.

Marguerite McBey
24, 25, 32, 33, 34, 38, 39, 45, 46, 47, 50, 55, 56, 61, 62, 68, 69, 70, 72, 73, 74, 81, 82, 83.

Joe McPhillips
26, 44.

Private Collection, photograph courtesy of The Fine Art Society.
67.